100%

GET THE WHOLE PICTURE

ENERGY AND FUEL

PAUL MASON

Cavendish Square

Published in 2024 by Cavendish Square Publishing, LLC
2544 Clinton Street, Buffalo, NY 14224

First published in Great Britain in 2020 by Wayland

Website: cavendishsq.com

Series editor: Elise Short
Produced by Tall Tree Ltd
Editor: Lara Murphy
Designer: Jonathan Vipond

Picture Credits
t-top, b-bottom, l-left, r-right, c-center, front cover-fc, back cover-bc
Shutterstock: 1tl, 9tl, 13cl, 15cl MicroOne, 1tr Puripat Lertpunyaroj, 1br, 5t Gyuszko-Photo, 2, 3tr, 4br, 5br, 5bl, 31bl, 22-23 SkyPics Studio, 3ctr Budimir Jevtic, 3cbr, 18-19 tele52, 3br, 29br Presslab, 4bl Dmitry Sheremeta, 5br Enmaler, 6tl showcake, 6bl Photology1971, 7tr Jenson, 7cr EvrenKalinbacak, 7br Monkey Business Images, 8tl small smiles, 9br Lee Prince, 11c VanderWolf Images, 13t zhu difeng, 13bl Matt Gertson, 14tr Mark Agnor, 14-15b Voss Tau, 16-17 Aurora72, 16bl curraheeshutter, 17tr VectorMine, 19tr Mykola Gomeniuk, 20bl Dario Lo Presti, 20br Bildwerfer_StephanG, 21tl Kostenyukova Nataliya, 21cr Diyana Dimitrova, 21br Dzianis_Rakhuba, 22tr SanderMeertinsPhotography, 22-23 SkyPics Studio, 22bl mantisdesign, 22br Tilman Ehrcke, 24cl, 25cr Puripat Lertpunyaroj, 25t Studio BKK, 26bl Neamov, 27t Oleksandr Derevianko, 27bl Andrea Izzotti, 28tl BlueRingMedia, Creative Commons: 29br NASA/Goddard Space Flight Center Scientific Visualization Studio United States Geological Survey

Cataloging-in-Publication Data

Names: Mason, Paul.
Title: Energy and fuel / Paul Mason.
Description: Buffalo, New York : Cavendish Square Publishing, 2024. | Series: 100% get the whole picture | Includes glossary and index.
Identifiers: ISBN 9781502668639 (pbk.) | ISBN 9781502668646 (library bound) | ISBN 9781502668653 (ebook)
Subjects: LCSH: Power resources--Juvenile literature. | Fuel--Juvenile literature.
Classification: LCC TJ163.23 M376 2024 | DDC 333.79--dc23

CPSIA compliance information: Batch #CSCSQ24: For further information contact Cavendish Square Publishing LLC at 1-877-980-4450.

Printed in the United States of America

Find us on

CONTENTS

All measurements in this book are presented in metric, as they are the units most scientists prefer to work in.

Energy and fuel

Energy is often described as "the ability to do work," and it is found everywhere, from tiny atoms to massive machines. We use energy all the time and we need huge amounts of it.

In 2018:

85%
OF THE WORLD'S ENERGY WAS GENERATED FROM FOSSIL FUELS

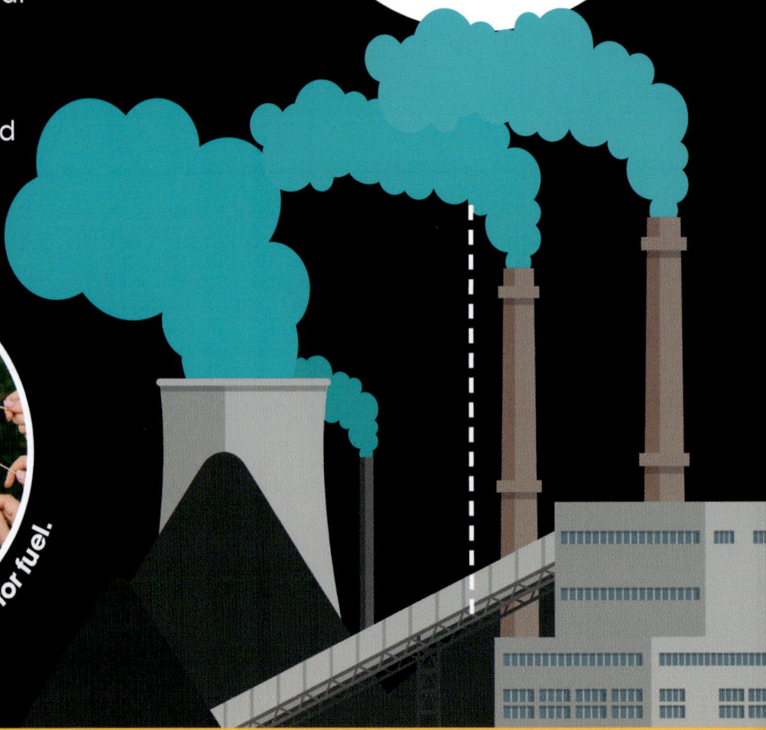

Fuel

In the past, the word "fuel" described something that could be burned to produce energy in the form of heat.

Today, "fuel" is also used to describe other sources of energy.

A campfire uses wood for fuel.

Fossil fuels

The three main fossil fuels are coal, oil and natural gas.

They were formed over millions of years from the decayed remains of plants and animals.

Fossil fuels will one day run out, so they are called nonrenewable.

Renewables

Renewable energy sources include hydropower (power made from water), wind, solar and geothermal energy (made from the heat of the Earth). They will never run out.

11%

CAME FROM RENEWABLES

Nuclear

Nuclear power comes from splitting uranium atoms, which releases huge amounts of energy.

People disagree over whether nuclear energy is renewable.

- ✔ For: The world has a 1,000-year supply of uranium, which is effectively limitless.
- ✖ Against: Uranium WILL one day run out, and nuclear energy leaves behind harmful by-products, unlike other renewables.

4%

WAS PRODUCED BY NUCLEAR SOURCES

13,820 MTOE

AMOUNT OF ENERGY THE WORLD USED IN 2018, MEASURED IN MTOE (MILLION TONNES OF OIL EQUIVALENT)

One TOE is the amount of energy contained in one tonne of oil.

Energy use

The world's demand for energy gets greater all the time. Between 2018 and 2040, the world's energy use is predicted to increase by 25 percent.

Energy footprints

A person's energy use is sometimes called their "energy footprint."

- An energy footprint is made up of ALL the energy one person uses.
- It includes not only obvious things, such as charging phones, but also energy used to make clothes and other possessions.

In 2020, world energy use was approximately:

Residential energy use includes heating, cooling, lighting, cooking and entertainment.

8%
RESIDENTIAL

Other uses of energy include agriculture, where energy is used to make fertilizers and pesticides and to heat greenhouses.

28%
OTHER USES

3,164,000,000 tonnes of oil equivalent

AMOUNT OF ENERGY USED BY THE WORLD'S BIGGEST USER, CHINA, IN 2018

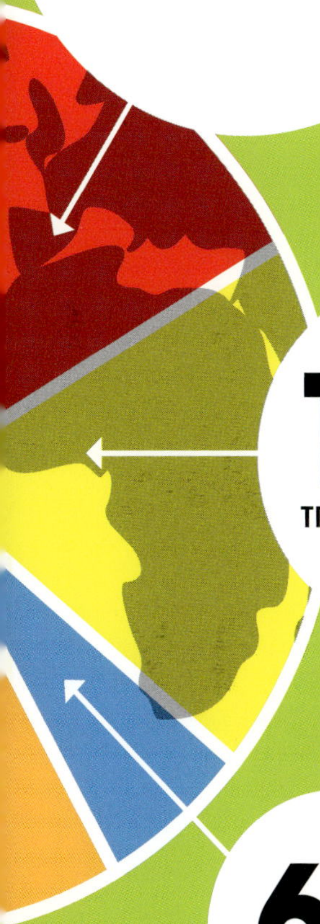

39%
INDUSTRIAL

Industrial energy use includes making products and materials, such as the aluminum a car is made from or the glass of a cell phone screen.

19%
TRANSPORTATION

Transportation energy use is anything from powering a car or bus to a plane, train or ship. It can be for transporting people or goods.

6%
COMMERCIAL

Commercial energy use is similar to residential energy, but it happens in shops and offices.

Each person in China used as much energy as you would get from **2.27 tonnes of oil.**

In the U.S. that same year, each person used the equivalent of **6.9 tonnes of oil.**

Despite the U.S. using more energy per person, China is the biggest energy consumer due to its huge population and developing infrastructure.

Fossil fuels

The world's energy comes mostly from fossil fuels. There are three types: coal, oil and natural gas.

Ancient energy

Fossil fuels contain the energy stores of ancient plants and animals. Burning them releases this energy as heat and light.

Coal is made from fossilized plants.

In 2018, 85 percent of the world's energy came from fossil fuels.

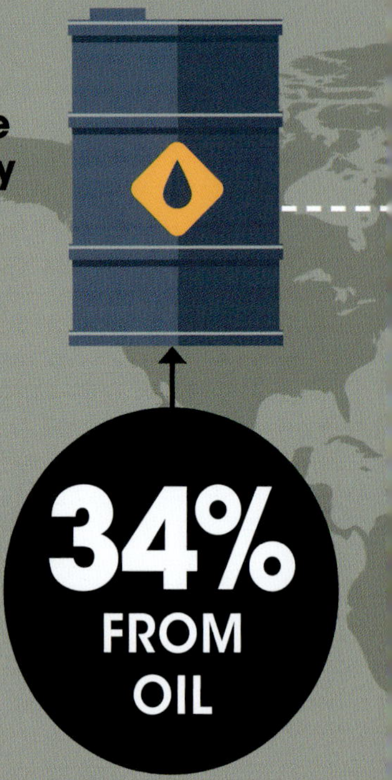

Fuel formation

Fossil fuels formed from the remains of plants and animals that died millions of years ago.

1. Dead plants and animals are buried in mud or water and do not decay.

2. Over millions of years, heat and pressure turn them into oil, gas or coal.

3. Today, these fossil fuels are being extracted and used.

Greenhouse planet

Surrounding Earth is a layer of gases called greenhouse gases, including water vapor, methane and carbon dioxide. They trap some of the sun's heat and keep Earth warm.

Burning fossil fuels releases more greenhouse gases into the atmosphere. The amount of greenhouse gases is building up and Earth is getting too warm. This is called global warming.

66%

INCREASE IN THE AMOUNT OF THE GREENHOUSE GAS CARBON DIOXIDE (CO_2) PRODUCED BY BURNING FOSSIL FUELS BETWEEN 1970 AND 2011

27% FROM COAL

24% FROM NATURAL GAS

15% FROM NON-FOSSIL FUELS

Global warming effects

- Polar ice caps and glaciers are melting, causing sea levels to rise and seaside areas to flood.
- Sea temperatures are rising, killing coral reefs and affecting ocean plants and animals.
- Our weather is becoming more extreme, with more violent storms and droughts.

a melting glacier

Electricity

How many times a day do you use electricity? Every time you use your phone, fridge, heating, laptop, and much more. Electric-powered items are a huge part of our lives.

Clean or dirty?

You may not be able to see the pollution caused by using electricity, but this doesn't necessarily mean that it is a "clean" form of energy.

It can be produced using a variety of different energy sources, but most electricity is produced by burning fossil fuels.

In 2017:

38% OF THE WORLD'S ELECTRICITY WAS PRODUCED BY BURNING COAL

23% CAME FROM NATURAL GAS

10% FROM NUCLEAR POWER

9% FROM OTHER RENEWABLES

IN TOTAL, **65%** OF THE WORLD'S ELECTRICAL ENERGY CAME FROM FOSSIL FUELS.

OVERALL, ABOUT **25%** OF GREENHOUSE GAS EMISSIONS COME FROM ELECTRICITY PRODUCTION, SO ELECTRICITY IS NOT THAT CLEAN AFTER ALL.

Coal to electricity

Coal is the world's main source of energy for making electricity.

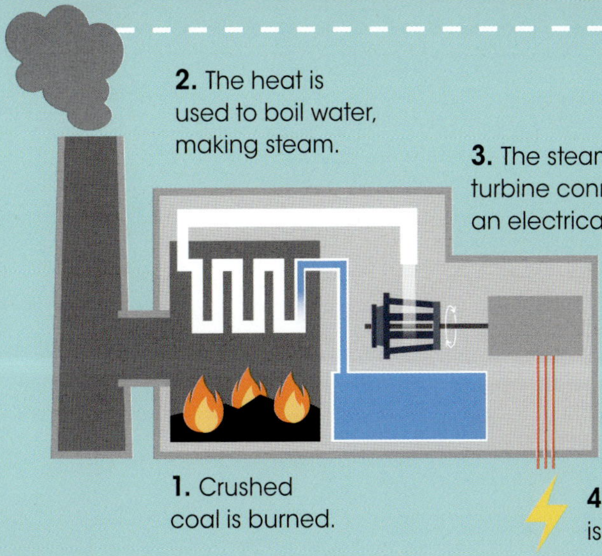

The biggest polluter

Burning coal releases more carbon dioxide than any other fossil fuel.

- Coal releases almost twice as much carbon dioxide as natural gas.
- It releases over a third more carbon dioxide than petroleum.

clouds of smoke from a coal-fired power station

16%
FROM HYDROPOWER

4%
FROM OIL

37.1 gigatonnes

ESTIMATED AMOUNT OF CARBON DIOXIDE RELEASED INTO THE ATMOSPHERE IN 2018.

This is a rise of about 2.7 percent from the previous year, making them the highest levels recorded in history. More than 70 percent of the demand growth (more people using more energy) was met by burning oil, natural gas and coal.

Oil

The world depends on oil. It provides energy for cars, boats, trains, planes and other vehicles. Without oil, our transportation systems would grind to a halt.

In 2018, most of the world's oil reserves were located in 14 countries.

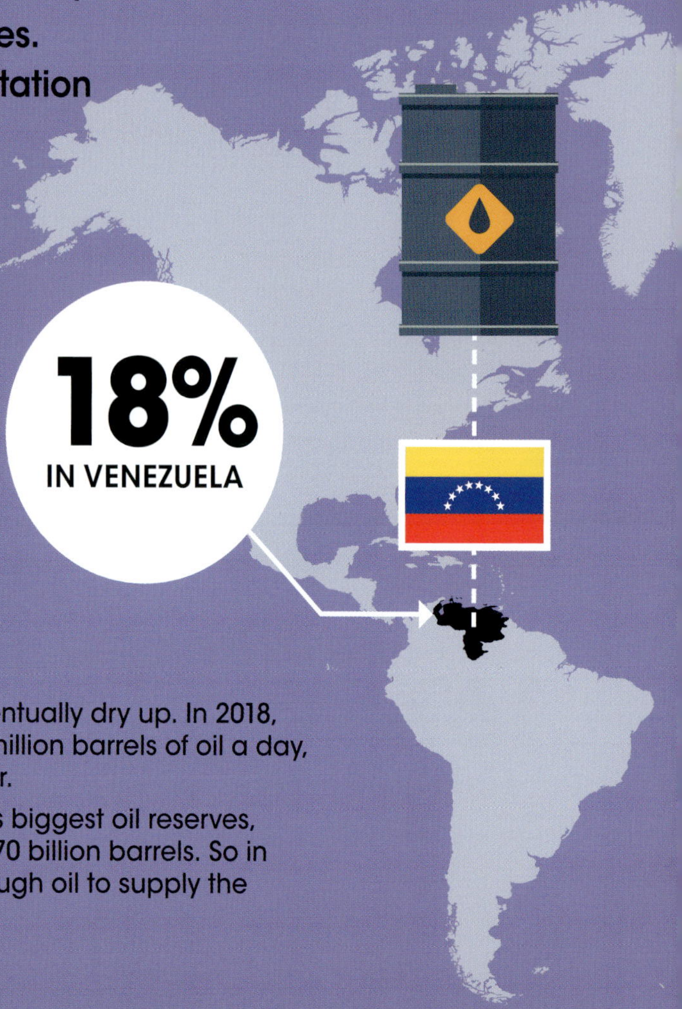

Running out of oil

Our supplies of oil will eventually dry up. In 2018, the world used over 100 million barrels of oil a day, which is 36.5 billion a year.

Venezuela has the world's biggest oil reserves, estimated in 2018 to be 270 billion barrels. So in 2018, Venezuela had enough oil to supply the world for 7.4 more years.

465,000,000 barrels

AMOUNT BY WHICH THE WORLD'S DEMAND FOR OIL HAS BEEN RISING EVERY MONTH FOR THE LAST 10 YEARS

This is the same as an extra 1 million barrels of oil per day, every day.

Iran
The first Middle Eastern oil well was dug in Iran in 1908. In 2019, Iran produced **2,225,000** barrels of crude oil per day.

an oil well

9%
IN IRAN

57%
HELD BY 11 OTHER COUNTRIES

16%
IN SAUDI ARABIA

Saudi Arabia
Saudi Arabia is the world's biggest exporter of oil. In 2016, it sold **US$161,000,000,000** of oil to the rest of the world.

Oil can be extracted from under the sea.

Inaccessible reserves

At the moment, not all oil reserves are worth extracting. They are buried too deep or are in inaccessible places.

As oil begins to run out, its price will rise. It may become worth spending money to bring these inaccessible reserves to the surface, but this will have an environmental impact.

Coal

Coal is one of our most important energy sources. It provides much of the world's electricity. People also burn coal for heating, and it is widely used in industries such as steelmaking.

An open-cast mine can be seen above ground.

an underground mine

Mining coal

Coal was formed from the remains of plants deep underground, millions of years ago.

Over time, some layers of rock where coal is found have moved. In some places, the coal can now be dug out right at the surface.

Other coal reserves are still found deep underground. Some mines are a kilometer below the surface.

Where does the world's coal come from? In 2016:

45% WAS MINED IN CHINA

9% WAS MINED IN THE U.S.

9% WAS MINED IN INDIA

There are **four key types of coal:**

- anthracite
- bituminous
- sub-bituminous
- lignite

Some are less polluting than others. Even the cleanest—bituminous coal—releases 93.3 kg CO_2/million Btu (British thermal unit).

Coal vs. oil vs. gas

Coal is the most polluting fossil fuel.

Coal is responsible for 43 percent of carbon dioxide emissions from fuel combustion.

36 percent is produced by oil.

20 percent is produced by natural gas.

231,000,000 TOE

AMOUNT THAT WORLD COAL PRODUCTION REDUCED IN 2016 DUE TO ENVIRONMENTAL RESTRICTIONS

This was a fall of 6.2 percent compared to the year before.

China's production fell by 7.9 percent.

The U.S.'s production fell by 19 percent.

How much is left?

Coal is the most abundant of the three fossil fuels. In 2016, experts thought we probably had:

115 years' worth of coal

50 years' worth of natural gas

50 years' worth of oil

7% WAS MINED IN THE EU

7% WAS MINED IN AUSTRALIA

23% WAS MINED IN OTHER COUNTRIES

Natural gas

Natural gas is the second most important fuel for energy. In 2018, it provided 24 percent of the world's energy.

Gas uses

- We burn natural gas in our homes, shops, restaurants and offices for cooking and heating.
- Natural gas is also burned to produce electricity.
- In industry, natural gas is used to provide heat for making glass, steel, bricks, cement, paper and many other things.
- Industry also uses gas as an ingredient when making fertilizer, plastics, drugs and fabrics.

In the U.S. in 2018:

34% OF NATURAL GAS WAS USED IN ELECTRICITY PRODUCTION

34% WAS INDUSTRIAL

Gas extraction

Natural gas is extracted by drilling down to underground gas reserves. A concrete-and-metal pipe is put down the hole, as well as a pump at the surface.

After being brought to the surface, the gas is cleaned of water and other impurities that would stop it from burning well.

Fracking

Natural gas can be extracted from some rocks using a process called fracking. Fracking is unpopular. People don't like that it makes the ground unstable and pollutes water.

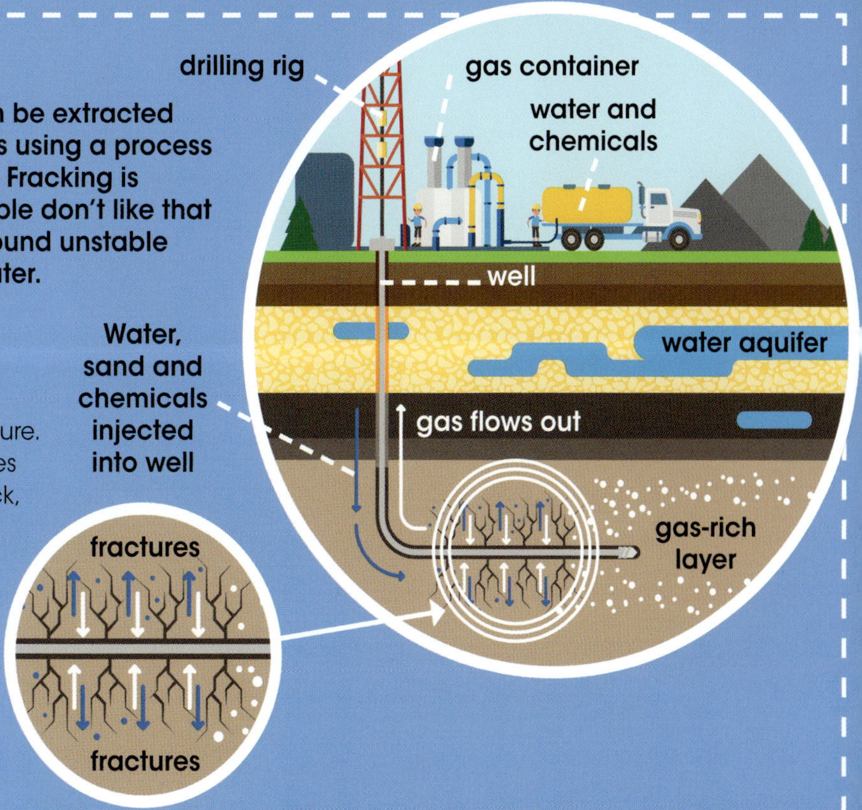

Under pressure

Chemicals are pumped into the rock at high pressure. This creates fissures (cracks) in the rock, releasing gas.

17% WAS RESIDENTIAL

12% WAS FOR COMMERCIAL USE

3% OTHER

The cleanest fossil fuel

Natural gas is the cleanest fossil fuel. It produces about half as much pollution as coal. However, gas is still not a clean fuel.

FIFTY TIMES MORE CO_2 IS RELEASED WHEN USING NATURAL GAS TO PRODUCE ELECTRICITY THAN WHEN USING WIND ENERGY.

Hydropower

Hydropower harnesses the energy of water flowing downhill. It is currently our main source of renewable energy.

58%
OF THE WORLD'S RENEWABLE ENERGY COMES FROM HYDROPOWER

Renewable hydro

Earth's gravity means water will always flow downhill, so hydropower should last forever.

Major source

Hydropower provides almost one-fifth of the world's total electricity.

River power

- Hydroelectric power comes mainly from rivers.
- The downhill flow of water makes turbines (like the steam-driven turbine on page 11) spin at high speed. The turbines drive electrical generators.
- Hydropower stations are often found in mountainous areas, where the rivers flow fast.

42%
COMES FROM BIOENERGY*, GEOTHERMAL, SOLAR, AND WIND POWER

*renewable energy from plant or animal sources, such as wood or dung

103,100,000

NUMBER OF MEGAWATT HOURS (MWH) OF ELECTRICITY PRODUCED IN 2016 BY THE ITAIPU HYDROELECTRIC DAM IN SOUTH AMERICA (RIGHT)

One MWh is enough energy to power about 330 homes—so Itaipu could produce enough energy for more than **34,000,000,000** homes.

The Itaipu Dam lies between Brazil and Paraguay.

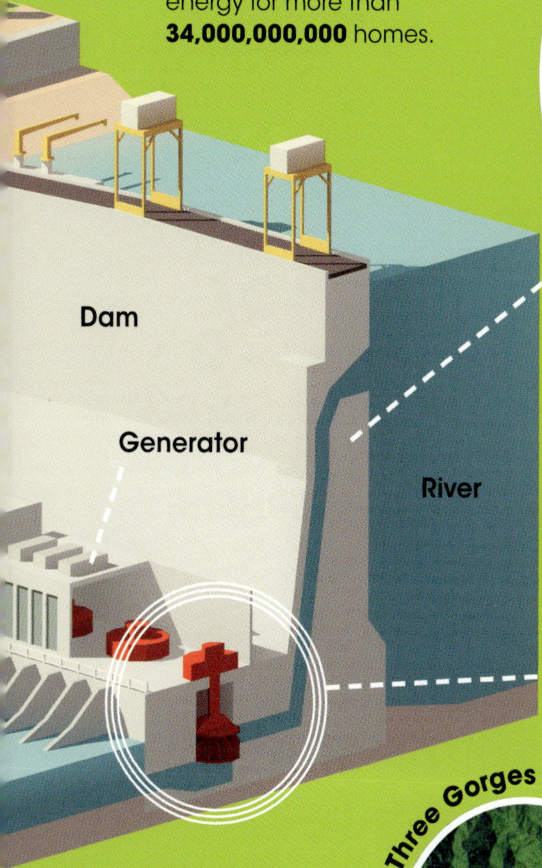

Dams

In many hydroelectric projects, rivers are dammed to hold back lots of water. This stored water can be released whenever electricity is needed.

Turbines

These are sent spinning as water flows past them.

Flooded lands

The lakes behind hydroelectric dams cover large areas of land. The people who once lived there had to move. Animals and plants lost their homes or drowned.

Three Gorges Dam, China

Before the dam

This satellite image shows the Yangtze River before the dam was built.

After the dam

This image shows the flooding after the dam was built.

Solar power

In the history of our planet, most energy originally came from the sun. Even coal, for example, is the remains of ancient plants that grew using the sun's energy.

30%
OF SOLAR ENERGY IS REFLECTED BACK INTO SPACE

70%
OF SOLAR ENERGY ENTERS EARTH'S ATMOSPHERE

Solar-powered weather

Solar energy is absorbed by Earth's oceans and landmasses.

Temperature differences are created, and when air moves from cold to hot areas, it causes wind.

Solar energy also drives the water cycle, forming clouds that bring water to the land.

Water in the air condenses to form clouds.

Direct sunlight

Humans have always used direct sunlight as a form of energy. For example, it dries wet clothes, heats rooms and warms water.

174 Petawatts

THE AMOUNT OF SOLAR ENERGY HITTING THE EARTH AT ANY ONE MOMENT. THAT'S 174,000,000,000 MEGAWATTS, WHICH IS ALSO 174,000,000,000,000,000 WATTS (1 MEGAWATT = 1 MILLION WATTS).

Using your phone for 3 hours a day uses about 5 watts, so 174 Petawatts is enough energy for **104,400,000,000,000,000** hours of phone use.

Solar electricity

Solar energy can be converted into electricity using photovoltaic cells.

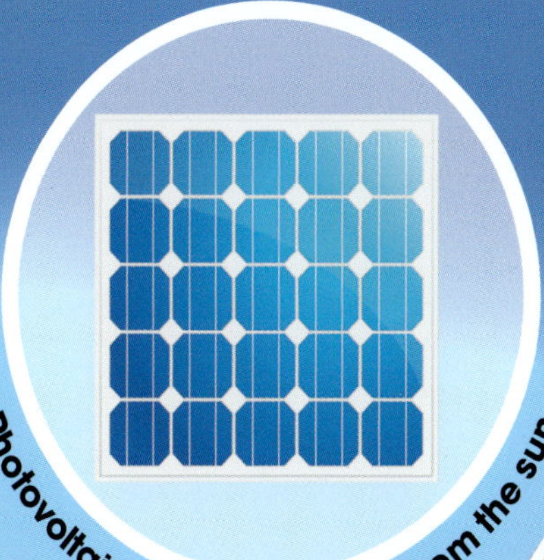

Photovoltaic cells absorb light from the sun.

Some people put solar panels on their home.

Solar-powered home

Solar panels can be fitted to the roofs of homes and businesses, providing clean, renewable energy for the people inside.

Massive solar farm

The world's largest solar farm is in the Tengger Desert in China. It covers 1,200 km^2 and can produce a maximum output of 1,500 megawatts of electricity at any given time.

THE AMOUNT OF ELECTRICITY WE GET FROM SOLAR ENERGY IS GROWING RAPIDLY. BETWEEN 2010 AND 2016 IT WENT FROM 50,000 MEGAWATTS PER YEAR TO 305,000 MEGAWATTS.

Wind power

People have been using wind energy since at least 5,000 BCE, when wind-powered boats sailed up and down the Nile River in Africa.

old windmills in the Netherlands

Windmills

Around 4,000 years ago, people in Persia and China began using windmills to grind grain. Today, modern versions of these windmills, called wind turbines, turn wind into electricity.

Wind power

Today, about one-third of the world's countries use wind power to provide electricity for their national grid (a network of high-voltage power lines).

Wind turbines

The turbines work by using the wind to turn propeller blades. This turning movement then powers an electrical generator, which converts mechanical energy into electrical energy.

Wind farms

A wind farm can be made up of dozens of wind turbines. Wind farms are often sited on or near coasts because this is where winds are most reliable.

onshore wind farm

offshore wind farm

Euro wind
In the EU, over 10 percent of electricity comes from wind turbines.

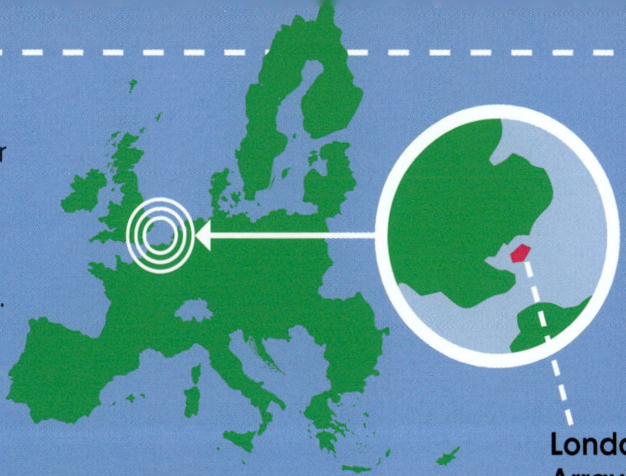

THE WORLD'S BIGGEST OFFSHORE WIND FARM, THE LONDON ARRAY, CAN PRODUCE ABOUT 2.5 MILLION MWH OVER A YEAR, CAPABLE OF MEETING THE POWER NEEDS OF 600,000 HOMES.

The European country Denmark is the world leader in wind energy. In 2017:

41% OF DENMARK'S ELECTRICITY CAME FROM WIND POWER

33% CAME FROM OTHER RENEWABLES

26% CAME FROM FOSSIL FUELS

107 meters

LENGTH OF EACH BLADE ON THE HALIADE-X, THE WORLD'S BIGGEST WIND TURBINE

That's the same length as a football field!

Geothermal energy

Geothermal energy is one of the few kinds of energy that does not come from the sun. Instead, its source is deep in the Earth.

Heat from the core

At the Earth's core, there is a great store of heat from when the planet was formed. Today, radioactivity within the center adds to this heat.

a plume of water from a geyser

The amount of geothermal energy accessible within just 10 km of the Earth's surface is far greater than the total amount of energy contained in all the oil and gas reserves worldwide—but it's not accessible everywhere. This energy sometimes produces powerful jets of boiling water that erupt as geysers.

Of the total energy found near Earth's surface from both sources:

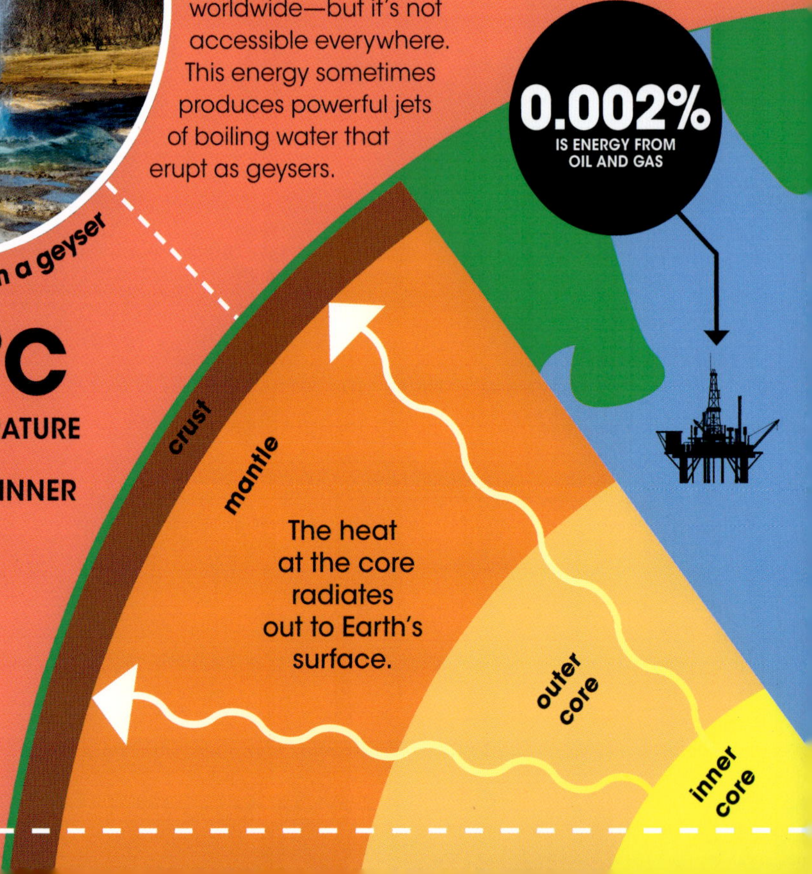

6,000°C

ESTIMATED TEMPERATURE AT THE BOUNDARY BETWEEN EARTH'S INNER AND OUTER CORE

That's as hot as the surface of the sun.

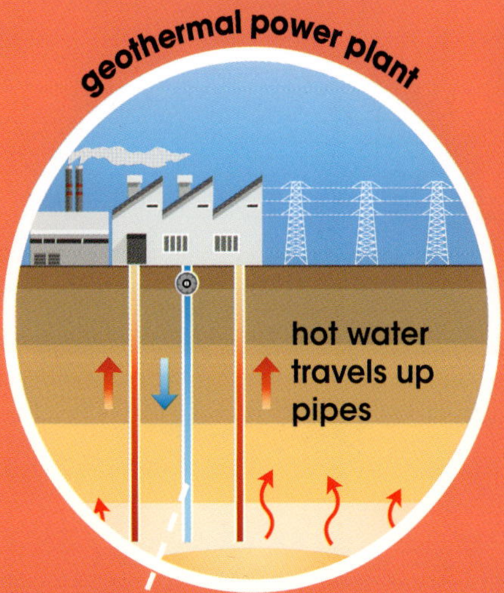

cool water is returned

Geothermal electricity

Geothermal heat can be used to power turbines and electrical generators.

- Steam production wells are drilled deep into the Earth. Natural hot water is brought to the surface through pipes, where it turns to steam and is used to spin turbines.
- The Geysers geothermal power station in the U.S. is the world's largest and can provide electricity for almost 1 million homes.

geothermal swimming pool

Geothermal heating

In Europe, 3,731 towns and cities have geothermal heating systems.

Located on one of Earth's major fault lines, Iceland can access vast underground reserves of geothermal energy.

In Iceland, 87 percent of homes have geothermal heating. Geothermal energy is also used to keep roads clear of ice and to heat public swimming pools and pavements.

99.008%
IS GEOTHERMAL ENERGY

Is geothermal energy really renewable?

Underground rock is capable of providing heat for many decades. However, it may eventually cool down, making it impossible to generate energy.

Wave and tidal power

Wave and tidal power both use the energy contained in moving seawater, but they work in different ways.

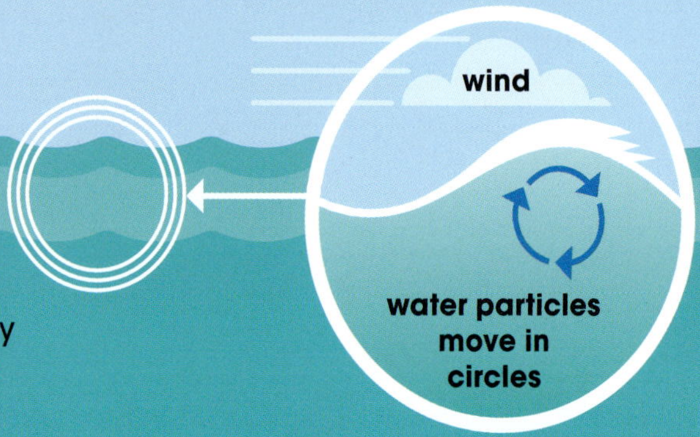

Wave power

Wave power contains energy from winds that blow across the ocean. The energy travels across the sea in the form of waves.

Wind makes the ocean surface choppy as it passes over. Water particles move in circles, producing waves on the surface. These waves, packed with energy, travel along the water toward the shore.

Wave power problems

Harnessing wave power is difficult. Waves are so powerful that they can smash up the equipment.

Wave energy tends to arrive in spurts, so to be useful, the energy has to be stored using large batteries.

16,000,000,000

ESTIMATED NUMBER OF HOMES THAT COULD BE POWERED BY THE WAVE ENERGY REACHING U.S. SHORES EACH YEAR

Some coal and oil power stations only convert about 30 percent of the fuel's energy into electricity. Tidal power is far better.

80% OF TIDAL ENERGY IS CONVERTED INTO ELECTRICAL ENERGY

Tidal power

Tidal power comes from the twice-daily rise and fall of the oceans. It is more predictable and easier to harness than wave power.

20% IS LOST, MAINLY BECAUSE OF FRICTION

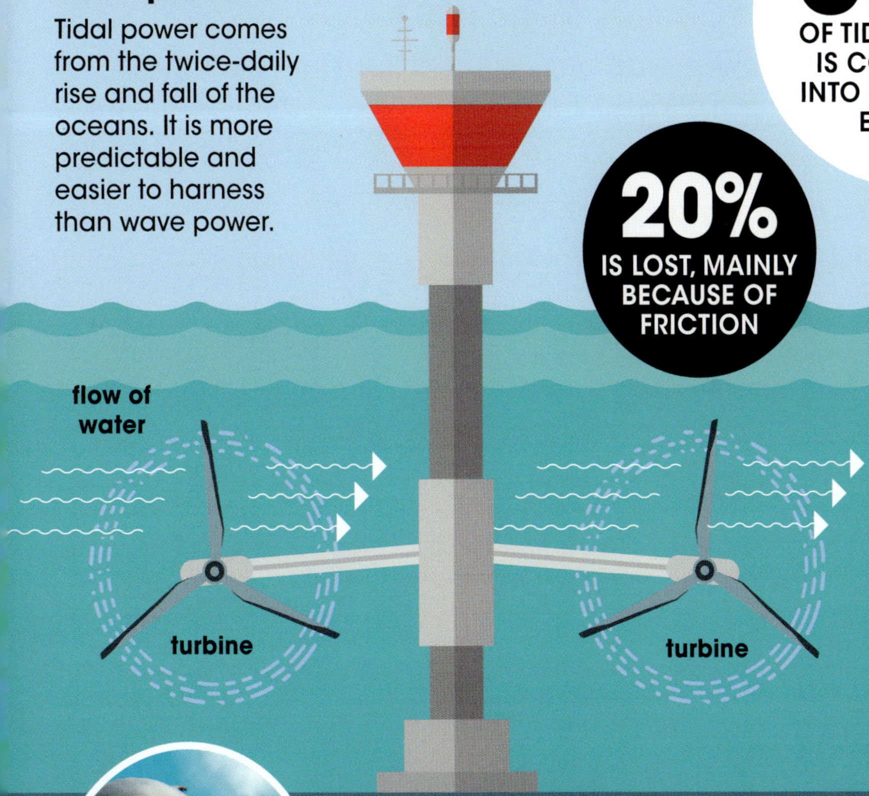

The turbine can be turned to face the tide when it starts to flow the other way.

Blades spin as water flows through. This movement is used to power generators.

Tidal difficulties

Tidal power stations are expensive, compared to other types of renewable energy.

The turbine blades can also harm sea life.

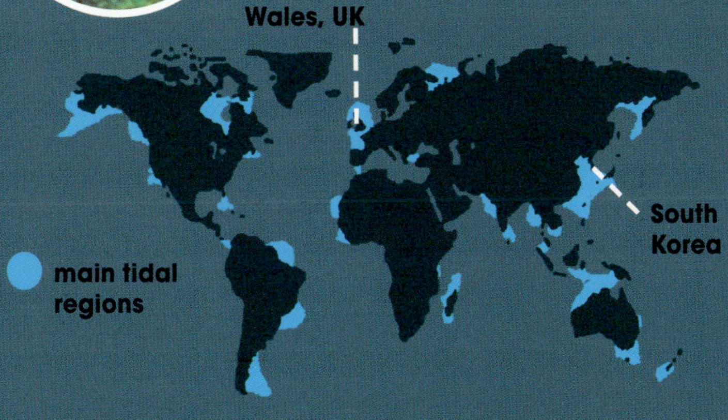

Some of the biggest tidal power stations include the Sihwa Lake Tidal power station in South Korea and the proposed Swansea Bay tidal lagoon project in Wales, UK.

Nuclear power

The first nuclear power plant began to produce electricity in 1954 at Obninsk in the USSR. By 2016, nuclear power was providing about 11 percent of the world's electricity.

Why not have nuclear power?

Today, 31 countries have nuclear power stations. Most countries do not use nuclear energy because nuclear power stations can be expensive to construct, complicated to maintain, and very dangerous if anything goes wrong.

How it's made

Nuclear power comes from a process called nuclear fission.

1.
A uranium atom is split, releasing huge amounts of heat.

This process produces dangerous radioactive waste, which has to be sealed away, usually in underground chambers.

2.
The heat turns water into steam.

3.
The steam drives a turbine and an electrical generator.

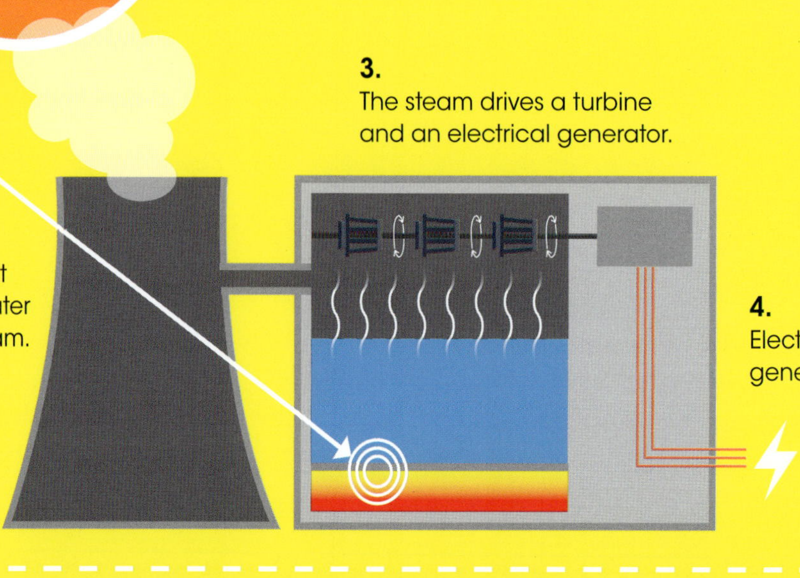

4.
Electricity is generated.

Many countries are nuclear-free because they fear a nuclear disaster.

16% OF THE WORLD'S COUNTRIES HAVE AT LEAST ONE NUCLEAR REACTOR

Nuclear countries

In 2018, four countries relied on nuclear energy for at least half of their electricity.

France 71.7%

Slovakia 55%

Ukraine 53%

Hungary 50.6%

31 NUMBER OF PEOPLE KILLED AFTER EXPLOSIONS AT THE CHERNOBYL NUCLEAR PLANT IN 1986

Experts think about **4,000** people will eventually die as a result of contamination from the radiation that was released. It is thought that the area won't be safe for humans to live in for at least **20,000** years.

84% OF THE WORLD'S COUNTRIES ARE NUCLEAR-FREE

Fukushima disaster

In 2011, a tsunami damaged the nuclear power station in Fukushima, Japan. Experts think hundreds of people may eventually die due to the radiation that was released.

testing the soil for radioactive pollution

Glossary

atmosphere
The layer of gases that surrounds a planet. Earth's atmosphere is mostly made up of the gas nitrogen, with some oxygen and small amounts of other gases, including carbon dioxide and argon.

BTU
Stands for "British Thermal Unit." It is a unit of heat that is defined as the amount of heat needed to raise the temperature of one pound of water by 1°F (Fahrenheit).

carbon dioxide
A colorless gas that is released by living things when they produce energy. It is also released by chemical reactions, such as burning fuel, and is a major greenhouse gas in the atmosphere.

combustion
The act of burning something. It usually involves the combination of heat, fuel, and oxygen.

core
The center of the Earth. Earth's core is divided into an inner and an outer core. The inner core measures about 2,440 km across, and the outer core stretches out about another 1,000 km.

crust
The thin outer layer that covers Earth. It ranges in thickness from 5 km to 50 km and makes up just 1 percent of Earth's total volume.

decay
When something, such as a dead body, breaks down into simpler parts.

energy footprint
This refers to the amount of energy that a person or group uses for all of their activities.

fertilizers
Chemicals that are spread over plants to help them grow. Fertilizers are used to improve the amount and quality of a crop grown on farms.

fossil fuel
The term used to describe a fuel that has been formed from the remains of long-dead living things. Fossil fuels include coal, oil, natural gas and peat.

fracking
A method of extracting oil and gas from rocks by pumping water and chemicals under high pressure into the rock to force the oil and gas out.

generator
A device that converts one form of energy into another, usually mechanical energy (from a spinning turbine) into usable electrical energy.

geothermal energy
Energy that is produced using heat from underground.

geyser
A hole in the ground that shoots out jets of hot water and steam from underground.

global warming
The gradual rise in Earth's temperature caused by an increase in carbon dioxide and other greenhouse gases in the atmosphere.

greenhouse gases
The name given to the group of gases that trap energy from the sun in Earth's atmosphere, heating the atmosphere up and causing global warming.

hydropower
The production of power using moving water. Hydropower includes hydroelectric dams on rivers, tidal power stations near coasts and wave power stations out at sea.

infrastructure
The word used to describe the network of facilities used by a group of people or a country. It includes roads, railways, telephone networks and power supplies.

mantle
The area inside Earth that lies between the core and the crust. Huge swirling currents

inside the mantle's semisolid crust push and pull on the crust above, breaking it up into huge pieces called tectonic plates.

nonrenewable
Something that cannot be replaced. Nonrenewable energy sources include coal, natural gas and oil.

nuclear fission
The splitting of an atomic nucleus, usually by the impact of another atomic particle. This process releases huge amounts of energy and can start a chain reaction where more and more atomic nuclei are split. It is used to produce power in a nuclear power station.

oil reserve
The amount of oil left to be extracted in a particular region.

open-cast mine
A type of mine where the mineral is dug out of the ground from an open pit.

pesticides
Chemicals that are sprayed on plants to protect them from plant and animal pests.

photovoltaic cell
A device that converts energy from sunlight into electric power.

radiation
A form of energy, such as heat, that is given off by an object.

renewable
Something that can be replaced. Renewable energy sources include solar power, hydropower and wind power.

solar farm
The name given to a large collection of solar power cells that produce electricity using sunlight.

turbine
A wheel made out of angled blades, which is sent spinning by the movement of flowing water, steam or wind. Turbines are connected to generators to produce electricity.

wind farm
The name given to a large collection of wind turbines.

FURTHER INFORMATION

Books to read
Eco STEAM: The Energy We Use
Georgia Amson-Bradshaw (Wayland, 2018)

Fuelling Up: Energy, Global Warming and Renewables
Rob Colson (Wayland 2017)

Renewable Energy
Harriet Brundle
(Kidhaven, 2018)

The exhaustive *Powered Up!* series of books by Theresa Morlock (PowerKids Press, 2018)

Places to visit
Fort Worth Museum: Science and History
1600 Gendy Street
Fort Worth, TX 76107
This museum features an exhibit about the different types of energy sources that are available in Texas.

Maryland Science Center
601 Light Street
Baltimore, MD 21230
Visit the Power Up! exhibit to learn all about how electricty powers the objects in your home or school.

National Museum of Nuclear Science & History
601 Eubank Boulevard SE
Albuquerque, NM 87123
Learn about the past, present and future of nuclear energy.

HOW TO READ BIG NUMBERS

1,000,000,000,000,000,000,000,000,000,000 = one nonillion
1,000,000,000,000,000,000,000,000,000 = one octillion
1,000,000,000,000,000,000,000,000 = one septillion
1,000,000,000,000,000,000,000 = one sextillion
1,000,000,000,000,000,000 = one quintillion
1,000,000,000,000,000 = one quadrillion
1,000,000,000,000 = one trillion
1,000,000,000 = one billion
1,000,000 = one million
1,000 = one thousand
100 = one hundred
10 = ten
1 = one

Index